IMAGES OF WALES

AROUND
LLANELLI

T0346824

IMAGES OF WALES

AROUND
LLANELLI

BRIAN DAVIES

The History Press

Frontispiece: The Llanelly and Mynydd Mawr Railway with Old Castle Tinworks on the right and Old Castle Pond on the left, *c.* 1957. The crowds walking along the railway are on their way to a see a rugby match at Stradey Park. The pond was created in the nineteenth century to provide water for the tinplate works. It was affectionately known as *Pond Twym* (Warm Pond), and was one of a number of industrial ponds in the Llanelli area where goldfish had bred. In the 1950s children fished for these goldfish with home-made rods of bamboo and floats made out of cut corks with matchsticks through them.

First published 2004
Reprinted 2004

Reprinted with revisions in 2008 by
The History Press
The Mill, Brimscombe Port,
Stroud, Gloucestershire, GL5 2QG
www.thehistorypress.co.uk

Reprinted 2014

British Library Cataloguing in Publication Data.
A catalogue record for this book is available from the British Library.

ISBN 978 0 7524 3370 7

Typesetting and origination by
Tempus Publishing Limited.
Printed and bound in England.

Contents

Acknowledgements 6

Introduction 7

one Buildings and Streets 9

two Trade and Industry 35

three Transport and Communications 53

four Religion 67

five People and Events 81

Acknowledgements

When I first started working on this book in 1998 Carmarthenshire County Council's Cultural Services Manager was David Griffiths and the Llanelli Area Librarian was Richard Davies. I should like to thank them for allowing me to use numerous photographs from the outstanding archives of Llanelli Library. Also Richard Davies, Phillip Connell, Yvonne Jones and Jean Phillips have willingly helped with countless questions, fetched and carried boxes of archive material, brought bound newspapers, found books and helped in many other ways.

I also wish to thank Ann Dorsett, Senior Curator of Carmarthenshire County Museum, for all the help she has given, and the museum for permission to use photographs of important exhibits from the Parc Howard Museum, Llanelli.

I also thank Andrew Pearson, the Editor of the *Llanelli Star*, for his ready help in publishing a letter requesting information on Llanelli artists and for permission to use material from the *Llanelli Star*.

My thanks to the artist John Bowen for sending a very informative letter on Walter Cole and allowing me to spend hours with him discussing his work and that of other Llanelli artists. Also to Walter Cole's niece Dorothy Margaret Davies who wrote to me and allowed me to come to her home and talk about him. Also to Dr Andrew Richards who kindly sent me his excellent, unpublished work on John Bowen. Also to the late Tony Evans and his wife Kathleen who welcomed me to their home in the Bryn where we discussed his work and that of other artists at great length. Tony was a delightful man, full of humour, who was not only a very talented artist but had a vast knowledge of art history. I also thank Kathleen Evans for allowing me to use photographs from the album that Tony had put together of his exhibitions.

I should like to thank Graham Davies for the photograph of Arthur John Davies MM, and for access to the extensive research that he has done on the award of the Military Medal to this gallant Llanelli man. My thanks also to Arthur John's grandsons John Andrews and David Davies as well as Graham for permission to use this material in the book. John Andrews also supplied me with other photographs and information on his grandfather relating to his work as a postman in Dafen and a photograph and information on Dafen Cricket Club.

Many other people have helped me by allowing me to publish material or by assisting in in my research. I thank Ivor Bevan, Gwyneth Bevan, Brian Bradley, Sheila Bradley, Ena Davies, John Davies, Roger Davies (Llanelli AFC), Mair Edwards, Nigel Evans, Noel Evans, Elizabeth Freeman, Nora Griffiths, Terry Griffiths, Wayne Griffiths, Marion Hurford, Howard John, May John, Terry Jones, Shane Kelly, David Madden, Roy Miles, John Pellew, Margo Phillips, William Phillips, Irene Powell, Patrick Loobey, Eiry Reynolds, Brian Richards, Glenys Stone, Derek Warry and Nevil Williams.

My thanks to my daughters Ruth and Rebecca who gave great encouragement and support. Ruth spent many hours digitally enhancing some photographs that were otherwise too damaged for publication and transformed them into excellent images.

My thanks to John Edwards and John Westland who read the text and made valuable suggestions.

Introduction

Compiling and researching this book has been a great pleasure because it has afforded me the opportunity to return regularly to the town in which I was born and grew up, to walk around the places that I loved as a boy, and to meet old friends and make many new acquaintances. It has also been tinged with sadness because so much of the old town that I knew has been demolished. Gone is the old Market Pavilion that was described in 1896 as one of the most magnificent buildings in Wales; it was there that my mother had a stall and I helped to serve as a young boy and teenager. Also gone are such lovely buildings as the old Grammar School (Yr Ysgol ar y Bryn) where I studied, much of the old hospital, a significant section of Stepney Street, including the impressive building of the York Hotel, the Hippodrome (Haggars) where, as a boy, I was transported for a couple of hours to exotic places, the Palace (Vint's), much of Market Street, a large part of the historic Buckleys Brewery, docks, tinworks and numerous other buildings. Moreover, a historic railway (the Llanelly and Mynydd Mawr) has been ripped up. Llanelli was so richly endowed with important buildings and, somehow, managed to lose so many of them. Time and time again the people I have spoken to in compiling this book have expressed sadness at the changes they have witnessed.

What I have tried to do in compiling this book is threefold. First, I have tried to put together a collection of photographs and ephemera that show something of the Llanelli that once was. While many beautiful and historic buildings have been demolished they live on in photographs and drawings. Secondly, it will be obvious from my selection of material that I have inclined heavily to photographs that put an emphasis on people. Whether it is Edwardian boys and girls standing smartly (and still) in the street while the photographers took their shots, whether it is tinplate workers, steelworkers, pottery workers, artists or whatever, I have put an emphasis on people. My selection of photographs of streets, for example, leans heavily towards what is described as animated street scenes. This is quite deliberate. Whilst lovely and historic buildings can be destroyed, the people that built them, lived in them or worked in them are those that made and created the history of Llanelli. They are the people whose character has shaped the town. Thirdly, however, I have brought these photographs up to the present time. My interest in the history of art, for example, means that I have included some of the important artists in Llanelli over the past seventy years such as Derrick Pratt, Walter Cole, John Bowen, Vernon Hurford and Tony Evans. They deserve recognition in writing and I hope this book will provide that in the limited space available.

In selecting photographs I have tried to show that for many people life in industrial Llanelli was not easy and I hope that something of that is captured in this book. My father, who was a tin worker, cycled all the way from Felinfoel to the Morewood's Works every working day and I never heard him complain. It was a way of life that was accepted. When I talked to him about this towards the end of his life he simply said 'It was hard, Brian, it was hard'. The fine Llanelli artist Tony Evans who is featured in this book and whose paintings powerfully captured life in the tinplate works and collieries, told me of an occasion when he saw someone with tears in his eyes at one of his exhibitions. When he asked him what was causing him such grief the man told him that he had worked in the tinworks and the paintings had reminded him of how hard it was. I hope that a number of the photographs used in this book will emphasise this hardship that existed not just in the industrial sphere, of course, but in other areas of work such as the dangerous and tiring work of the cockle pickers.

During the past two decades a number of excellent books have been published about Llanelli and I have gone to them repeatedly to confirm facts or to gain new information. John Edwards' books are an example of how to combine scholarly research with a readable prose as is David Griffiths' history of the Borough Council. The book *Tinopolis* that John Edwards edited contains informative and interesting articles on Llanelli's tinplate trade by a range of writers. William and Benita Rees' *Birth of a Town* is an excellent, well researched fund of information. I also benefited greatly from the writings of Michael Denman, Gareth Hughes, Howard Jones, John Nicholson, Richard Thomas, Herbert Board and Nevil Williams.

People's experiences are important and I have incorporated much of this in the text. It has been a pleasure to talk to people in homes and on the streets and keep notes of what they said. Time and again I have been met with interest and kindness and have learned so much from their experiences.

Many of the illustrations in this book are from postcards as these provide a rich source of photographic material for people interested in local history. The period from 1902 to 1914 has rightly been described as the 'Golden Age' of postcards for it was in these years that postcard collecting achieved a popularity that has never been exceeded. Postcards were produced on almost every conceivable subject and these were avidly collected and stored carefully in albums. Many of these cards survive and the interest in them over the past five decades has brought numerous collections to light.

Finally, it should be noted that in 1966, Llanelli Borough Council passed a resolution to change the spelling of the name of the town from 'Llanelly' to the Welsh form of 'Llanelli'. In this book, therefore, I have used the new form throughout except where the name is used in the name of historical companies such as the Llanelly and Mynydd Mawr Railway, and when 'Llanelly' is used in a historical context that demands the old spelling.

Brian Davies
June 2004

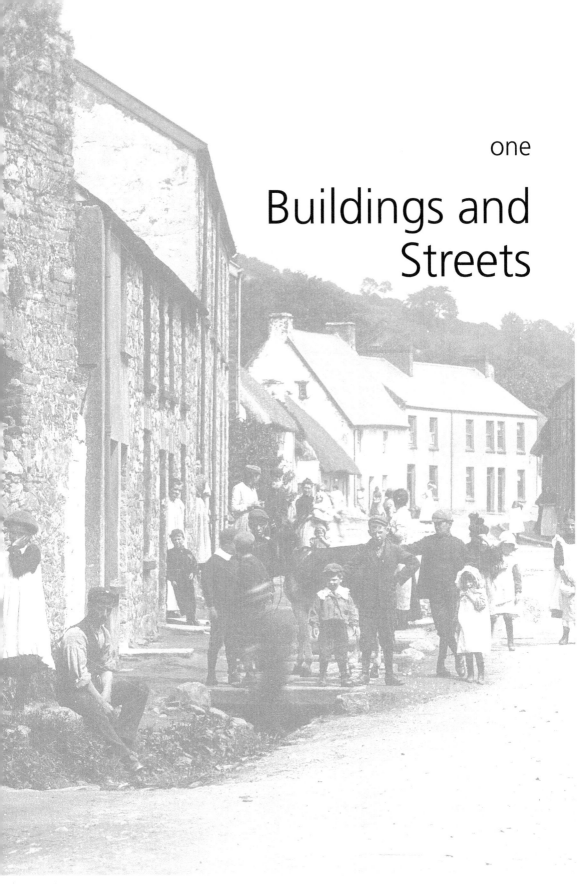

one

Buildings and
Streets

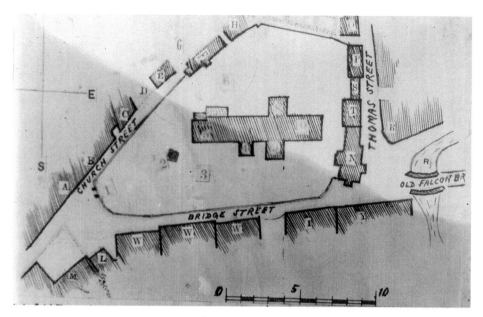

Map of Llanelli Parish Church and its surroundings, *c.* 1800. The buildings have been lettered and a contemporary hand-written key identifies the buildings. In Church Street it records the Mansel (A), The Ship Inn (C) and John Deer's house and shop from where John Wesley preached (D). Llanelli House is in Bridge Street (W), and, in Thomas Street, we see the location of the old Falcon Inn now London House (N), the Bear Inn which was once a Post Office (S), and Child's House, who was an agent for the Stepneys (P).

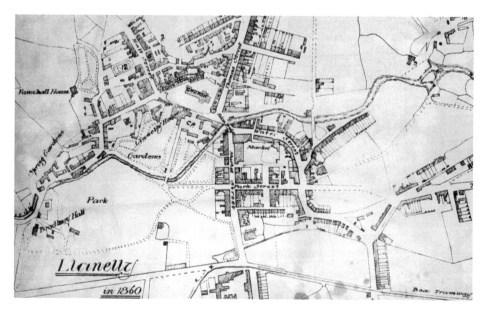

A map of Llanelli in 1860 traced by W.G. Price. This map shows how the town had expanded from the early part of the century but it is striking that the Parish Church is still at the heart of the town. The market was now located in the area bordered by Market Street, Water Street and Park Street.

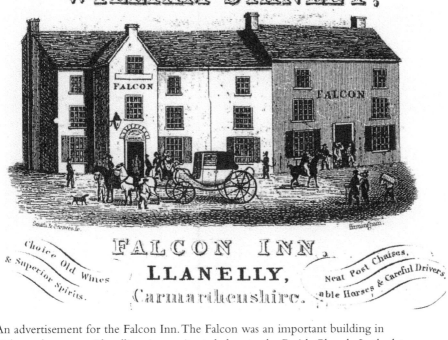

An advertisement for the Falcon Inn. The Falcon was an important building in eighteenth-century Llanelli, as it was situated close to the Parish Church. In the late eighteenth century it was acquired by the entrepreneur Henry Child who was the founder of the brewery that later became known as Buckley's Brewery. He started a business auctioning property, household and agricultural goods, and the auctions were held at the Falcon Inn.

London House, c. 1906. This is a view of London House – the old 'Falcon', which was situated on the bottom of Thomas Street.

A section of Llanelli churchyard looking towards Church Street, 1795. This is one of the oldest sketches relating to Llanelli showing the churchyard in a neglected state with the old cross broken. The Ship Inn and other premises would be built later, where the cottages stand in this drawing.

The Parish Church and Church Street, *c.* 1905. At the turn of the twentieth century concern was expressed at the state of the church, which had fallen into disrepair. Restoration commenced and the formal opening of the restored church took place in January 1907. In the Edwardian period numerous views of the church were produced as postcards.

A painting of the market in front of the Parish Church, commissioned by James Buckley, c. 1850. It must rank as one of the most important records of the mid-nineteenth century Llanelli Market. In front of the church entrance goods such as stockings, shoes and earthenware items are being sold. An early description of the painting says that the man on horseback is a young James Buckley, talking to Squire Chambers and his wife. A little nearer is Davy Thomas the Town Crier with a bell in his hand. Note the man in the stocks under the notices on the wall to the right of the gate. The trees on the right are in front of Pemberton House, which later became the location of the Athenaeum. Further along is Llanelli House which at this time was inhabited by William Chambers.

Llanelli, 1854. Llanelli had a number of very talented amateur and professional painters who recorded the town at different stages in its history. This particular view of the town was painted in 1854 by a Mrs Harvard, the wife of a Wesleyan minister, who was a resident in the town. Mrs Harvard made many sketches of the town, which are now of great historical interest and an enterprising local stationer had a number of her sketches engraved by Rock and Co., London, and published them for sale as letter page headings. This sketch shows part of Bigyn Hill. Near the centre is Erw Colliery which was also known as Little Old Castle. The Parish Church is also conspicuous.

Above: The Athenaeum, *c.* 1920. The Athenaeum building was erected in 1857 and the adjoining Nevill Memorial building in 1866, both buildings being financed by public subscription with rich and poor contributing. The official opening ceremony of the Athenaeum, chaired by W.H. Nevill, was held on 25 January 1858. The building had to be equipped with furniture and fittings and a ladies committee undertook to raise money by organising a bazaar. This event took place on Friday 25 September 1857, and raised the grand total of £140. In 1860 the Llanelly Mechanics' Institute and its small library moved to the Athenaeum. This institution had been located in the schoolroom behind the Old Park Street Congregational Chapel where it held a stock of books which people had access to after school hours. In 1897 there were debates in the Mechanics' Institute about the implementation of the Free Library Act and, in January 1898, the act was adopted in Llanelli. A Saturday was chosen for the formal transfer to the Urban District Council and the new free library was crowded with readers.

Opposite above: A 1911 watercolour of Llanelli Parish Church and Bridge Street by Alfred Edward Parkman, one of the most accomplished artists to visit and paint in Llanelli at the turn of the twentieth century. Born in 1852, he was the son of Henry Spurrier Parkman a Bristol portrait painter. Early in his life he painted views in and around Bristol, but, later, towards the end of the nineteenth century, he moved to Swansea. Although he is best known for his outstanding watercolour drawings of places around the Gower Peninsula he did a number of watercolour drawings of Llanelli.

Opposite below: Vaughan Street, *c.* 1895. The street was named after the Vaughans a powerful and influential family in and around Llanelli. Margaret Vaughan married into the Stepney family.

Stepney Street, 1896. With the rapid development of the town in the nineteenth century and the change in location of the market, Stepney Street began to develop as a major street. By 1876 a local newspaper reported that commerce appeared to be centralising itself and that old tradesmen were establishing their businesses within the square of Market, Stepney, Vaughan and Bridge Street. The name of the street commemorated the Stepney family and the Stepney estate.

A postcard of Stepney Street, *c.* 1912. In the Edwardian era, when postcards were eagerly sought after, many of the cards sold in towns were views of various streets. For present-day collectors of old Llanelli postcards the views of Stepney Street are by far and away the most common street scenes that are found, indicating the importance of the street at that time. This view of Stepney Street is by the Cardiff photographer Ernest T. Bush, who took a number of high quality photographs in the Llanelli area.

Murray Street, 1896. On the right is Greenfield Baptist Chapel, built in 1858. The name of the street commemorated the family estates (in Ireland) of the Murrays. In 1823, Euphemia Jemima Murray, the daughter of General John Murray of Queen's County Ireland, married John Stepney Cowell.

Murray Street, April 1958. In the distance on the left is the Palace Cinema, known to local people as Vint's. It was built by Leon Vint and opened in 1911 with a seating capacity for 1,000. In the 1960s it was converted into a Bingo Hall and remained like that until it was destroyed by fire in 1973.

Station Road looking north towards the town centre, *c.* 1912. On the immediate right is the shop of T. Brabyn Davies, ironmonger. It is interesting to see two boys with the hand held cart of M.B. & Co. Ltd. Such carts of different tradesmen would have been a common sight at this time. Many street names in Llanelli have historical significance. The road was formerly known as Salamanca Road commemorating the Battle of Salamanca fought in June 1812, in which John Stepney Cowell took part. It was appropriate, however, that the main road from the town centre to the station should be renamed Station Road.

Station Road looking south towards the station, *c.* 1910. On the right is WH Smith & Son with their display board hanging on the front advertising high class stationery, die-stamping and engraving.

Custom House Bank, 1938. On the right is the Cornish Arms, which was renamed the Bucket and Spade. The old name of the public house reflected the relationship of Cornwall to Llanelli. Many vessels and mariners came to the Seaside docks and many Cornish families had settled in Llanelli. Custom House Bank was renowned for its bare-knuckle fighters, and official and unofficial boxing matches took place outside the public house.

Custom House Bank, c. 1930. Every port would have a Custom House and, in Llanelli, the houses alongside the one in Seaside gave way to the area being known as Custom House Bank.

Hall Street, *c.* 1958. Bevan and Roberts the ironmonger's shop is on the left and the Mansel Arms on the right. At the end is Hall Street Church. The old Town Hall was located on the right which gave the road its name.

Halfway, *c.* 1914. The original house of the Halfway Hotel was situated halfway between the tollgates of Pemberton and Capel Isaf. This gave way to the name of the house and the surrounding area.

Market Street, *c.* 1895. A crowd of adults and children are gathered in front of the camera. To the right we can see Newark's Glass and China Warehouse with its unusual French advertisement stating: *Marchand de Faience* (Seller of Crockery) on the wall.

Photograph by the Llanelli photographer Vaughan Evans, *c.* 1912. A number of postcards used in this book were printed by John Vaughan Evans who sold many high quality photographs showing life in Llanelli in the first part of the twentieth century, often printed under the title Vaughan Evans' Photographic Series. He also produced a number of early Edwardian postcards showing street scenes and general views of Llanelli when the images were printed in a light grey format.

Mill Lane, *c.* 1935. Below the wall on the left flows the River Lliedi and beyond it is the edge of Buckley's Brewery.

Mill Lane, *c.* 1935. This was the entrance to Mill Lane from Water Street.

Frederick Street looking towards Vaughan Street, showing the culverting of the River Lliedi, 1929. In the 1920s Llanelli suffered severe unemployment and, in February 1929, was designated a 'Distressed Area'. Government money was released for public works and this was used to create employment in the culverting of the River Lliedi from Vaughan Street to Town Hall Square.

Workmen culverting the River Lliedi under Spring Gardens, 1929. Spring Gardens and King Square were both demolished to make way for the new Broadway in Frederick Street leading to the Bullring with car parking spaces and the laying out of the new Town Hall Square Gardens.

Above: Town Hall Square, *c.* 1918. The magnificent building of the new Town Hall reflecting the prosperity of the town in late Victorian times was opened on 31 March 1896. It was built of local dressed stone in the free classic style of architecture. It was designed by the architect William Griffiths of Falcon Chambers, Llanelli, and the contract for building it went to T.P. Jones of Station Road at a cost of £11,000.

Below: King Square being demolished, 1929.

Above: Town Hall Square, with the central car park under construction, 1931. After the clearance of King Square the way was open for the construction of a car park to meet the needs of the growing number of people owning cars.

Below: Town Hall Square showing the new traffic roundabout, April 1939. To the left is the splendid building of the York Hotel. In the centre are the impressive buildings of the Lucania Billiard Hall. On the right is Moriah Chapel.

Top: Haggar's Theatre, Market Street, *c.* 1910. In the early 1890s J. Edmund Noakes opened the Royalty Theatre, which could seat 1,400 people. In June 1910, it was taken over by the Haggar family, headed by William Haggar, and the theatre became known as Haggar's Theatre. Under him came the heyday of provincial live theatre. In its time the theatre was to host many great stars such as G.H. Elliott, Marie Lloyd, Gracie Fields and Tom Costello. Charlie Chaplin came there before he became famous and, in 1951, a projectionist at the Hippodrome (as it had become known by then) used to take visitors to the disused dressing rooms and show them the door used by Charlie. The theatre had no bar facilities, but adjacent to it in Water Street, was the Angel Inn. In the interval between performances people could go into the inn for a drink and a bell above the bar was rung to let them know when it was time to return to the theatre.

Top: Hippodrome staff, performers and guests, *c.* 1920s.

Above: Popular Cinema, *c.* 1920. The cinema known locally as the Pop was on the old Fair Field, close to the Town Hall. It is interesting to notice that the entrance on the left from Old Castle Road was by way of a small bridge over the River Lliedi.

Opposite below: Hippodrome, October 1976. In 1915 the Haggar's family changed the name to the Hippodrome, though it was always popularly known as Haggars. During the bingo craze of the 1960s it was converted into a bingo hall. In 1977 this historic building was demolished along with much of Lower Market Street, to make way for a Tesco supermarket.

Llanelli Hospital, 1896. By the 1880s the expansion of the town's population had made the little hospital on the Bigyn totally inadequate and it was clear that a new building was urgently required. In October, 1884, the foundation stone was laid and the hospital opened in 1885. There was an emergency ward with four beds, and male and female wards with eight beds in each, making a total of twenty beds. The hospital also had an operating theatre.

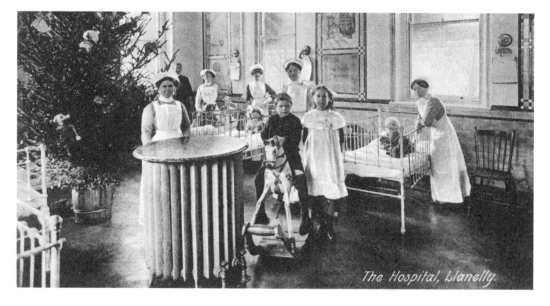

Llanelli Hospital children's ward, c. 1908. In 1903, Mrs Buckley, widow of the late Dr H.C. Buckley, made clear her intention of defraying the cost of building a children's ward at the hospital in memory of her husband Henry Child Buckley who had been the Medical Officer of Health in Llanelli. For this ward she commissioned a series of beautiful hand-painted Doulton tile panels showing various nursery rhymes and these have now been preserved in the new Prince Philip Hospital in Llanelli.

Above: Cowell Street looking towards Stepney Street, *c.* 1895. This view indicates how important Cowell Street had become by the late nineteenth century. A number of hand-held carts of merchants are seen on the left, and a tram makes its way down the tramlines in the centre of the road. The boys in the foreground are dressed in typical late Victorian dress and it is interesting to see that they all wear caps.

Right: Goring Road looking north, *c.* 1912. On the right is Hall Street Church with its Gothic style of architecture built by the architect James Wilson from Bath, who was the husband of Maria Buckley. The church was opened in 1856. Further up the hill, on the left, is All Saint's Church.

Kidwelly Castle, *c.* 1908. The castle, built on a steep ridge overlooking the River Gwendraeth, is an impressive example of Norman power. It is also a good example of castle development as it was altered on a number of occasions to take into account the latest thinking in military science.

Station Road, Kidwelly, *c.* 1906. The photographer has lined up the children and postal workers across the road from Kidwelly Post Office on the left.

Causeway Street, Kidwelly, *c.* 1908. The building in the centre has now been demolished, together with other buildings alongside, leaving a clearer view of the Town Hall further up the road. Immediately on the left is part of the wall of the Fisherman's Arms in Bridge Street.

Water Street, Kidwelly, *c.* 1906. A postcard by the Excelsior Company Ltd, Carmarthen, a company that produced outstanding photographic images of streets and views in Carmarthenshire. The photographer has gone to great lengths to get adults and children standing patiently along the street. An open ditch runs down the street, which possibly gave the street its name.

Loughor Bridge Opening, 24 April 1923. The official opening of the new bridge was greeted by huge crowds of people who gathered at both ends to watch the ceremony. Children from the neighbouring schools of both county councils were given a holiday to celebrate the event. The bridge, which linked up the two counties of Carmarthen and Glamorgan for vehicle and pedestrian traffic, replaced the old wooden structure that was considered unsafe.

Castle Street, Loughor, c. 1908. The Ship and Castle, on the immediate left, kept a horse and cart and part of the stables can be seen in the photograph. Originally the pub had a large front porch, but this was demolished. On the left is The Sanctuary, a building that dates back to the eighteenth century. In medieval times there was a sanctuary there, but little remains of this except an archway in the basement.

The Stores, Loughor, *c.* 1940.

Loughor Castle, *c.* 1906. In the early twelfth century the Normans extended their control over southern Wales and this castle was built at a strategic point overlooking a major river and link to the sea. The early castle was attacked and burned by the Welsh, but the Normans regained control and added several stone buildings. The rectangular stone tower that remains was built in the thirteenth century by William de Braose. This postcard of the castle is one of Raphael Tuck's cards.

Felinfoel, *c.* 1908. On the left is the Royal Oak Inn and in the distance is the old Felinfoel Mill.

Swiss Valley, *c.* 1912. The opening ceremony of the Cwm Lliedi Reservoir took place on
17 September 1878. Set in a picturesque valley the reservoir was nearly three-quarters of a mile
long and was estimated to hold 160 million gallons of water. Even though the weather was poor,
hundreds of people lined the embankments to watch the events. Cannons were fired and boats
carrying members of the board and friends went up and down the reservoir under the command
of Commodore Home, in his canoe, and Captain Thomas Jones, Harbour Master.

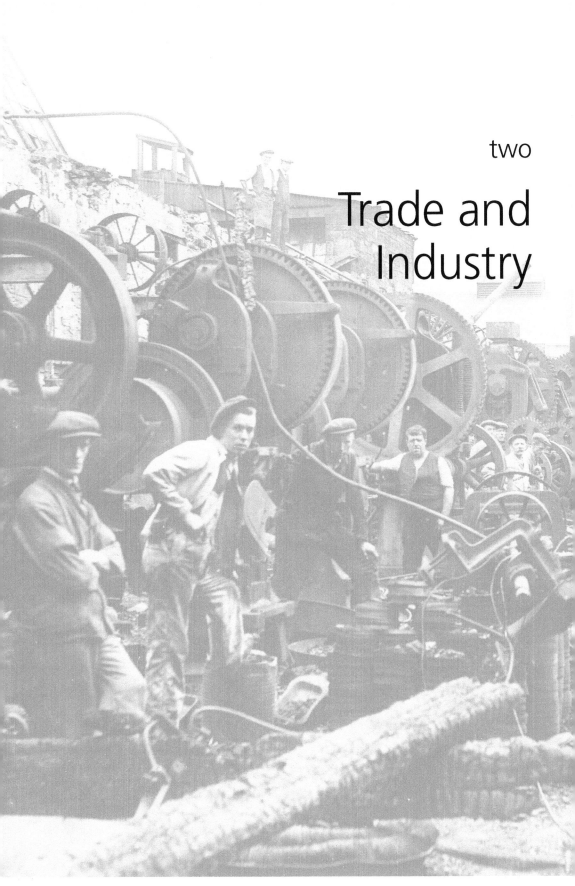

two

Trade and
Industry

Ashburnham Tinplate Works, Burry Port, *c.* 1910. Lord Ashburnham granted land near to the Burry Port Harbour to build the tinplate works. The foundation stone of Ashburnham Tinplate Works was laid by William Joseph Buckley JP of Penyfai, Llanelli, on 25 May 1889, and the works opened on 15 April 1890. Most of its finished product was exported from Burry Port Dock. The works closed on 2 February 1953.

Tinstamping Works, 1932. On 15 August 1932 a terrible fire demolished the Welsh Tinplate and Metal Stamping Co. Ltd. (popularly known as the Llanelly Tinstamping Works). This photograph, taken by the Llanelli photographer F.J. Anthony, shows men standing by the machine shop presses and gives an excellent picture of the arrangement of the machines within the works.

Kidwelly Tinplate Workers, *c.* 1900. Kidwelly was one of the earliest tinplate works in Britain having produced tinplate there since 1737. In tinplate production after the 'doublers' had folded and squeezed the metal into eight sheet packs and then cut them to the size required it was the job of 'openers' to separate the sheets of metal in the stacks. The openers were usually women who wore special gloves with a lead piece in the palm of the hand as, sometimes, sheets of metal stuck together. All the women are wearing thick gloves and aprons.

Llanelli steelworkers, 1893. These men are in the casting pits in front of the steam crane. Moulds were filled with molten steel, which became ingots. Once the ingots had solidified they were lifted out of the casting pit by the overhead crane before being transferred to the Mill Bay for rolling into 'tin bars.'

BUCKLEY BROS.

LLANELLY BREWERY

Above: An advertisement for Buckley's Brewery, *c.* 1890. The origins of the brewery lie in the late eighteenth century when Henry Child acquired land at the bottom of Thomas Street on which he developed a malting business. Henry Child had come to Llanelli from Pembroke to be an agent to Sir Thomas Stepney. He was an astute businessman with a wide range of interests in shipping, coal, milling and farming, and he also acquired the leases of several inns in Llanelli including the Falcon Inn at the bottom of Thomas Street. Under the influence of William Colley who was butler to Sir Thomas Stepney, and the town's leading Wesleyan Methodist, he became a Methodist. Later, his daughter Maria married an itinerant Methodist preacher, the Rev. James Buckley, who came to the town. Henry Child died in 1824 and his son, also Henry Child, continued as maltster though the business was operated by two sons of the Rev. James and Maria Buckley, Henry Child Buckley and James Buckley II. Henry Child died in 1831 and Henry Child Buckley died in 1836, and the business was then operated by James Buckley II. Under his guidance the business developed greatly and became the largest malting and brewing enterprise in the region.

Left: Buckley's Brewery lorries outside the Town Hall, *c.* 1910. This impressive fleet of lorries shows that Buckley's Brewery was doing well by the early part of the twentieth century.

Right: Griffiths & Son, architects and surveyors, with the entrance to Buckley's Brewery on the right, *c.* 1920.

Below: Felinfoel Brewery lorries, *c.* 1925. The Felinfoel Brewery had its origins in the King's Head in the village of Felinfoel which is said to have been an important coaching inn. David John, who had worked in coal mining and the tin plate industry became the licensee of this inn and, with the help of his family, he was able to produce fine beer. This beer was so good that it became very popular and he was able to sell it to other beer retailers. His prosperity was such that he was able to expand his business by building a fine stone brewery on the opposite side of the road in the grounds of his home, Pantglas, in 1878.

LLANELLY COPPER WORKS STACK.

Built in 1860-61 from plans by Mr John Bowen. It was 320 feet high, its internal diameter tapering from 33 feet at base to 9 feet at the top. 750.000 bricks were used in its erection. *(Vaughan Evans.)*

Left: Llanelli Copperworks Stack, *c.* 1912. For over a century the Stac Fawr (Great Stack) was a significant industrial landmark in Llanelli. It was even a landmark for incoming ships. Originally it was 320ft high but was shortened to just over 300ft. It was built to carry away the fumes from the Copperworks and its great height was to allow the fumes to go over Bigyn Hill. The Copperworks, which was built in 1805 by Charles Nevill and a consortium of other businessmen, was very important in Llanelli's development. In 1807, his son, Richard Janion Nevill was given a share in his father's partnership and, under his astute management, the Copperworks achieved great success. A common saying was that Nevill made the Copperworks and the Copperworks made Llanelli.

Below: Erw Colliery, *c.* 1888. The Erw Colliery, situated behind Old Castle Road, was opened in 1810. It was sunk to a depth of 120ft. It was owned by General Warde who owned several pits in the area but, by 1829, all of them had been taken over by R.J. Nevill as payment of a debt of nearly £30,000.

Above: Horeb Brick Works, *c.* 1910. The Blackthorn Brick Works Co. opened the brickworks known as the Eclipse or Horeb Brick Works in 1907 on the west side of the Llanelly and Mynydd Mawr Railway and close to the village of Horeb.

Below: A Sentinel lorry of the Llanelly Steam Haulage Co. operating for the Horeb Brick Works, *c.* 1930.

J.D. Rees, baker and confectioner, wholesale cake manufacturer, and sole agent for Bermaline Bread, *c.* 1908. The bakery was at No. 117 Station Road, as this postcard informs us. Such a postcard would have been used for advertising much in the same way as trade cards.

H.W. Lloyd, general draper, milliner and costumier, *c.* 1910. This was H.W. Lloyd's shop at Nos 41-43 Station Road. To the right is a horse-drawn wagon with the shop's advertisement displayed on the side. Lloyd also had another shop at No. 1 Robinson Street.

Above: Frank Bentley, ironmonger, No. 31 Murray Street, *c.* 1912.

Below: Frank Bentley's advertisement, *c.* 1912.

Telegrams:
Bentley, Ironmongers, Llanelly.

Telephone:
182 Llanelly

Frank Bentley & Son,

General Ironmongers.

Established 1896.

Works Requisites, Builders Hardware,
Electrical supplies,
Oils, Colours, Paint and Varnishes.
Tools for all Trades.

WE SPECIALIZE IN SHEFFIELD CUTLERY.

Agents for INGERSOLL WATCHES.

31, Murray Street,   Llanelly.

(Near Market Entrance.)

Farriers Arms, Cwmbach Road, *c.* 1906. This public house was situated on the main road from Llanelli to Trimsaran. It was close to the woollen mill known as the Cwmbach Factory.

Engine Inn, New Street, Burry Port *c.* 1925. The public house was built at the corner of New Street and Church Road.

Royal Exchange Hotel, *c*. 1895. The hotel was situated at the corner of Park Street and Market Street.

Employees of R.C. Jenkins, *c*. 1906. Robert Charles Jenkins was born in King Square, the son of a weaver. In 1904 he made an application for an off-license in premises known as the Cambrian Stores in Vauxhall, Llanelli, and was successful. An advertisement in a local paper in 1907 stated that he sold wines and spirits of the best quality at the lowest prices as well as Worthington and Evershed Ales, which could be delivered to any part of the town daily.

Ferryside cockle pickers, *c.* 1900. Cockle pickers were usually women and girls who wore ankle length skirts. Harvesting cockles was backbreaking work and it was dangerous because of the threat posed by the incoming tide. Also, the wet sand and mud left by the outgoing tide was treacherous as it was possible to be stuck in it like quicksand. The shells raked out of the sand would be packed into hand-made wicker baskets to be sold in local markets. Often a woman would carry a basket on her head and one on each arm.

Burry Port cockle pickers, *c.* 1910. The Burry Estuary has rich beds of cockles, which are found on the sand banks after the tide has gone out. For the cockle pickers the day would start as early as possible, depending on the tide, with the pickers following the tide out until they reached the cockle beds. Then the sand was raked to form mounds of cockles which were collected up and transported by donkeys or by cart.

Llanelli shrimpers, *c.* 1912. The shrimpers had their distinctive wide nets for sweeping the shallow parts of the Burry Estuary. Shrimps were sold in the local market or by people going around the houses. In the Machynis area Richard Thomas used to go round the area with his hand-held cart selling shrimps. He would call out 'Shrimps' and knock on the doors. Not surprisingly he became well known as Dic Shrimps.

Above: Bynea Post Office, Cwmfelin Road, 1937. To the right of the building is the area where trolleybuses used to turn. The building, which is now residential, is still there but the main road alongside was raised to create a gradual incline for the widening of Bynea Bridge.

Left: Post Office, Llanelli, *c.* 1911. In the Edwardian period a new Post Office was needed to meet the demands of an important industrial district like Llanelli. A local newspaper stated that the weekly mail had reached a figure of over 145,000 items. In 1911 the new Post Office was opened under the control of the postmaster William Phillips.

Above: Llangennech Post Office, 1921. This fine stone building housing Llangennech's Post Office was built in the 1880s when the sub-postmaster was Elias Richards. Later, around 1916, it was acquired by the Arnolds who purchased it in the name of their daughter Annie Jane. She married a schoolteacher Walter James Evans and, by 1921, was the sub-postmistress of the Post Office. She continued as the sub-postmistress until her death on 4 April 1966. Mrs Annie Jane Evans is on the left and, on her right, is her friend Miss May Jones.

Right: Pwll Post Office, Bassett Terrace, Pwll, *c.* 1912.

The old Market Pavilion under construction, 1894. The uncompleted pavilion allows us to see the splendour of its Victorian design with high central roofs supported on magnificent columns. When it was completed it was an outstanding example of Victorian architecture. In a historical note on Llanelli markets, H.A. Prescott wrote that the building was much admired, even in its own time when such erections were commonplace in Britain. It was generally agreed that there was no edifice of its kind to equal it in Wales and precious few outside the borders of Wales. Less than one hundred years later, the decision was taken to demolish it.

A fruit and vegetable stall in Llanelli Market, c. 1955. This stall was run by Annie Harries of Tanyrhodyn, Felinfoel, who has her daughters, Irene Powell and Maidie Bevan, on either side.

The Mill at Felinfoel, c. 1900. Felinfoel derives its name from the water mill which was built alongside the River Lliedi and opposite the White Hart Inn. Remains of the building can still be seen alongside the main road and features of the mill can be found by walking around the area by the river.

South Wales Pottery, c. 1912. In 1839 William Chambers Jnr began to build a pottery works in Llanelli next to the gasworks and on a site between Pottery Street and Murray Street. The South Wales Pottery was operating in 1840 and, by 1851, there were 123 people working there. In its time the factory had painters whose work has now become very collectable and sought after. These painters include Sarah Jane Roberts who painted cockerel plates, featured elsewhere in this book, and Samuel Walter Shufflebotham who worked at the factory for a short time.

1909
STEPNEY
WHEELS

(Patented in all Civilized Countries.)

ALL LONDON TAXIMETER MOTOR CABS ARE FITTED WITH
STEPNEY WHEELS

MANUFACTURERS :—

The Stepney Spare Motor Wheel Ltd.,

Telegrams : "Wheels," Llanelly.
Telephone No. 187.

Llanelly, Wales.

Branches : LONDON, BERLIN, &c.

For New and Improved Stepney Wheel see page 10.

An advertisement for Stepney Wheels, 1909. The invention of the spare wheel for cars took place in Llanelli in 1904 after T. Morris Davies' car had a puncture while driving to Brecon. It gave him the idea for a clamp-on wheel. He and his brother Walter had an ironmonger's business in the town, which had opened in 1895, and now they began to manufacture spare wheels with the company known as the Stepney Spare Wheel Co. The company grew rapidly and, in 1906, was floated on the stock market as a public company. In 1922, the company left Llanelli for London to be reformed as Stepney Tyres, based in Walthamstow.

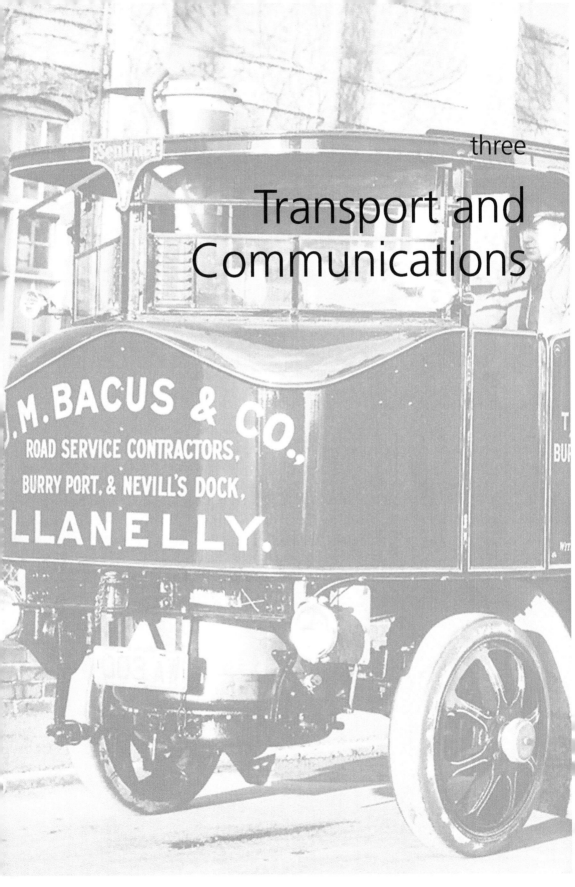

three

Transport and
Communications

Llanelli Station, 31 December 1899. This is the 4 o'clock express from London, which arrived at the station on the last day of the nineteenth century. This photographic image was used on postcards for years after the event.

Llanelli Station, c. 1912. The station is a fine example of Victorian architecture. After Swansea Station had been opened, the directors of the South Wales Railway decided to concentrate on laying a line to Carmarthen; this was opened in 1852.

Loughor Station, *c.* 1908. In the early part of the twentieth century a day's visit to the sands at Loughor was considered a great treat. Sometimes Sunday school outings went there. As the station was on the Great Western Railway, such visits could start at Llanelli Station.

Shunting at Llanelli Goods Yard during the Great Western Railway Strike, 1913.

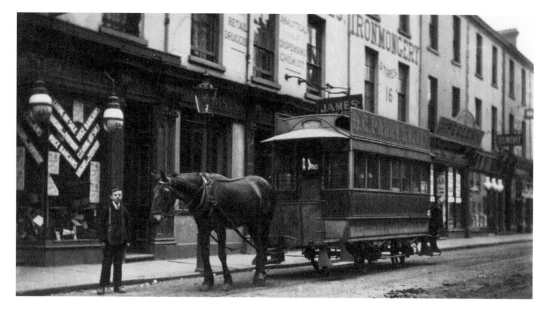

Horse-drawn tram in Stepney Street, *c.* 1900.

Horse-drawn tram of the Llanelly Tramways Co. Ltd, *c.* 1907. The tramway system opened on 28 September 1882, with three trams. This photograph was used on a variety of postcards in the Edwardian era and usually with a humorous caption such as: Go a long way in a long time. The postcard is captioned: The Llanelly Tramcar – The only amusement at Llanelly. The person who sent it to a friend in Holloway, London, in 1907, wrote on it that, 'These cars are famous through South Wales' and added that 'Llanelly, like Holloway, is still waiting for the electric trams'.

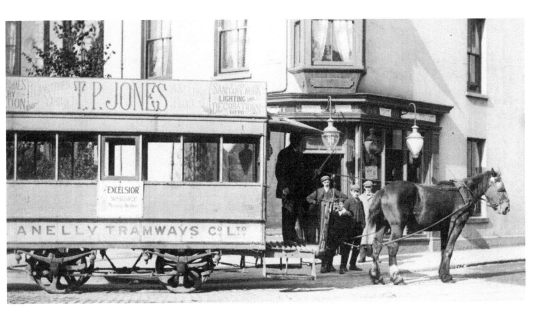

Llanelly Tramways Co. Ltd, *c.* 1907. The large advert at the top tells people to go to T.P. Jones in Station Road for sanitary work, lighting and decorations.

The Andrews Patent Omnibus, *c.* 1885. In 1883 the Llanelly Tramway Co. Ltd had competition when James Andrews introduced a new conveyance that was termed in the local press as Andrew's Patent Bus. This omnibus was adapted to run on the tramway rails and, curiously, the owners of the rails were legally powerless to stop the new company from using them.

Celebrating the opening day of the electric tram, 1911. The official inauguration of the Llanelly electric lighting and tramway system took place in 1911. An inspection was made of the power station after which electric trams conveyed the party over the system. Later, a luncheon was provided at the Stepney Hotel presided over by Mr Balfour of the firm of contractors.

A comic postcard produced by The Cynicus Publishing Co. Ltd that commemorated the first electric tram journey at Llanelli in 1911. This card would have been sold in shops in Llanelli soon after the event. Such a card could be captioned to suit a variety of such events, so was not produced exclusively for Llanelli. 'Cynicus' was a pseudonym for the artist Martin Anderson who was born in Scotland in 1854 and who, by the 1890s, had become recognised as one of the best caricaturists of the day. He saw the potential in the sale of picture postcards and the company he formed was very successful in the boom years prior to the First World War. Many of his cards, apart from this one, would have been sold in Llanelli.

Postcard showing the change in transport from the horse drawn to the electric tram, 1911. This postcard published by G.P. Frost of Llanelli was clearly intended to emphasise dramatically the change that had taken place in 1911.

Electric tram at Felinfoel, 1911. This postcard was posted in October 1911 showing that cards like this were on sale soon after the introduction of the new trams. In the background is the Union Inn with Felinfoel Brewery to the right.

An electric tram outside the Melbourne Inn, Station Road, *c.* 1912.

Above: An electric tram photographed by F.J. Anthony. Many of the photographs used in this book were taken and produced as postcards by Frank James Anthony (1877-1947). He was born in Llanelli and was a very gifted photographer. Early in the twentieth century he opened his photographic studio at No. 3 Vaughan Street, and remained there until 1939, when he moved his studio to Cowell House, where he remained until his retirement in 1947. Interestingly he was a friend of H. Mortimer Allen who was an outstanding Tenby photographer who produced many photographic postcards of his area. It is easy to imagine the two men discussing their work.

Opposite: Trams destined for Felinfoel and Llanelli Station outside Bradford House, Stepney Street, *c.* 1912.

The Burry Port and Gwendraeth Valley Railway locomotive *Mountaineer, c.* 1880. In 1858 a plan was drawn up to provide a railway line that linked the port in Burry Port with the Gwendraeth Valley. Building commenced in 1869. In 1870 this unusual Fairlie Patent double-bogie engine of the 0-4-4-0 type was used in a trial on the railway and remained in service for twenty years before being scrapped at Burry Port. Originally, when being built, it was known as *Pioneer* but became known as *Mountaineer* in service.

The Burry Port and Gwendraeth Valley Railway locomotive 0-6-OST type No. 5 *Cwmmawr* was built by Avonside in 1903 and was withdrawn in 1953. *Cwmmawr* was an appropriate name for one of the locomotives as, at first, the railway ran ten miles from Burry Port to Pontyberem, but was later extended three miles to Cwmmawr. The service also carried passengers from villages along the route.

The Llanelly and Mynydd Mawr Railway locomotive *Hilda* was an 0-6-OST type locomotive built by Hudswell, Clarke in 1917 and is, perhaps, the best known of the L&MM engines. In 1924 it was moved to Swansea East Dock Shed and acquired a bell for working on the quayside lines.

Railway Place, *c.* 1961.

North Dock, *c.* 1913. In the late nineteenth century it was clear that there was a need for improved dock accommodation in Llanelli. In 1895 the commissioners sought parliamentary sanction to construct a dock and other works in the port. The Bill passed through both Houses of Parliament and received Royal Assent in 1896. Work commenced on 15 March 1898, and was expected to be completed in two years, but serious disputes delayed the opening. Finally, the North Dock, built alongside the old Carmarthenshire Dock, was opened for commercial traffic in December 1903.

North Dock, *c.* 1937. The dock was 1000ft long and 400ft across, with an entrance 53ft wide. The dock was close to the Great Western Railway line and also to the Llanelly and Mynydd Mawr Railway.

Carmarthenshire Dock, *c.* 1900. The dock had its origins in 1799 when it was known as Squire's Dock or Squire Raby's Dock. Alexander Raby did well out of the Napoleonic Wars as he was making cannon and shot in his furnace (in the present Furnace area). He built a tram road that connected his furnace with his forge and collieries in the Morfa Bychan area, and this ran down to his shipping place in Seaside. Later, the dock became known as the Carmarthenshire Dock.

Great Western Dock, 1896. On 28 May 1833, the first stone of the entrance to a new floating dock was laid and the dock opened in 1834. It was known as New Dock but later this dock was taken over by the Great Western Railway and was known as the Great Western Dock.

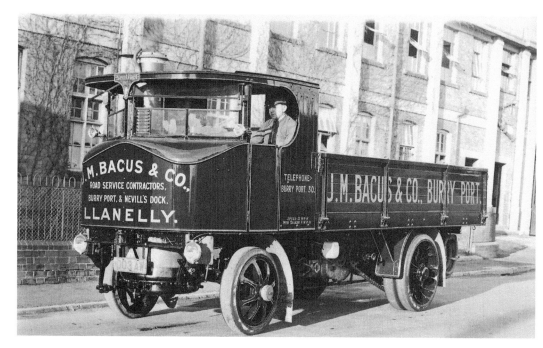

Sentinel lorry of J.M. Bacus and Co., road service contractors in Nevill's Dock, Llanelli, and in Burry Port, c. 1930.

Nevill's Dock Railway, 21 September 1962. The dock and railway served industries all over Llanelli. The little locomotives often crossed roads or went alongside houses so that their puffing and shrieking were commonplace sounds to many people.

four

Religion

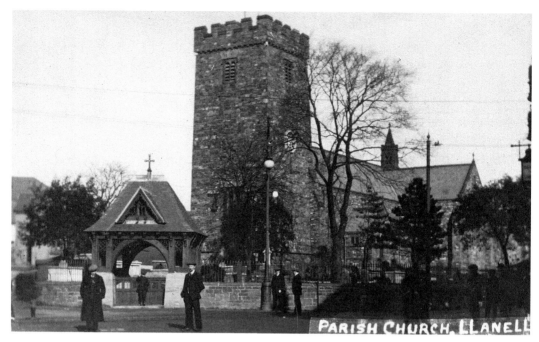

PARISH CHURCH, LLANELL

Above: The Parish Church, *c.* 1912. In 1911 a lychgate was erected by Arthur D. Davies to commemorate the rebuilding of the Parish Church. Arthur Davies was the local Registrar of Births, Deaths and Marriages.

Left: A South Wales Pottery bust commemorating John Wesley, *c.* 1840 to 1855. It was appropriate that the South Wales Pottery should produce a bust of the great itinerant eighteenth-century evangelist John Wesley as he preached several times in Llanelli. He was welcome at Llanelli House that was owned by Sir Thomas Stepney because Sir Thomas Stepney's butler, Wilfred Colley, was a Wesleyan Methodist. With the permission of Sir Thomas, Colley was allowed to hold preaching services in the kitchen of the mansion.

Above: All Saints Church, Goring Road, *c.* 1900. This church was designed by G.E. Street and was consecrated in 1874. Three years later it was enlarged, but owing to lack of money, the intended spire was never built. It was built on land given by Rees Goring Thomas of Llannon.

Right: Evan Roberts, 1904. The most well-known name in the Welsh Revival of 1904 was that of Evan Roberts. He began his working life as a collier at the Mountain Colliery, Gorseinon. Later, he worked at the Broad Oak Colliery, Loughor, until 1902, when he decided to learn the blacksmith's trade and was apprenticed to Evan Edwards, his uncle, at Pontardulais. It was while he was working at Pontardulais that he felt the need to leave secular work and so he gave up his job having decided to devote himself entirely to preaching.

Edna and Alwyn Jones, 1946. In 1946 Edna and Alwyn Jones, who were members of the Evangelistic Hall left Llanelli to become missionaries in the West Indies. They were to remain there until Alwyn's death in 1985. He was buried in Port of Spain, Trinidad. Edna returned to Llanelli where she died in 2002.

Moriah Baptist Chapel, Station Road, c. 1906. The Foundation Stone of Moriah was laid by John Powell, mason, in April 1870, in a service with the opening reading and prayer given by the Rev. J.R. Morgan minister of Zion Chapel. The reading, appropriately, was from 2 Samuel Chapter 7 and the Rev. Price of Aberdare delivered an interesting address on the chapter.

A river baptism in Felinfoel, 1913. Public baptisms in Felinfoel took place in the Baptismal Pool in the River Lliedi that flowed through the village. At the time of the Welsh Revival the Rev. Benjamin Humphreys conducted ninety-two baptisms there on one Sunday in 1905. Generally, the river flowing from Swiss Valley was shallow, but baptisms could take place in the village in the deeper part of the river created by the weir just beyond the point where the river flows under the road. This was a perfect place for such public baptisms and was also close to Adulam Baptist Chapel, Felinfoel. In the 1940s and 1950s it was also an excellent place for village children to spend many happy hours with their home-made equipment of jam-pots tied with string, which they used to catch minnows and sticklebacks.

Emmanuel Baptist Chapel, New Dock Road, c. 1906. Around 1906 the Llanelli photographer F.J. Anthony produced a series of postcards of chapels and churches in Llanelli, adding the distinctive feature of the ministers' portraits (inset in a circular frame) four of which are reproduced in this book. The foundation stone of the chapel was laid on 15 May 1894, by William Joseph Buckley JP, of Penyfai, and Elizabeth Wedge of Penyfai.

Tabernacle Chapel, Coleshill Terrace, *c.* 1906. This is one of the most magnificent buildings in Llanelli. The architect was John Humphries of Morriston who designed some of the largest chapels in Wales. A local newspaper described it as in the Italian style of the plain Corinthian variety with semi-detached pillars in front and that its Corinthian pediments were relieved by numerous arches and dressings. It was designed to hold one thousand people. The Memorial Stone was laid on Good Friday, April 1873, by Lady Stepney. The chapel was an offshoot of Capel Als which had already been responsible for the founding of Siloh Chapel, Seaside, Bryn Chapel and Park Congregational Church.

Calfaria Chapel, Ann Street, *c.* 1906. In 1880 a doctrinal difference resulted in about seventy members leaving Zion Chapel and founding Calfaria. The building on the right was the original place of worship but the church prospered and the larger building on the left was built to accommodate the increased congregation. In October 1901, the chapel was crammed to overflowing when Lloyd George came to give an address on the war in South Africa. It was estimated that there were about 1,100 people in the main building and 500 in an overflow in the vestry.

Zion Chapel, Upper Park Street, *c.* 1906. The origins of Zion Chapel go back to the late eighteenth century, around 1776, when some members of Adulam Chapel, Felinfoel, established a branch in the town with meetings being held in a house in Spring Gardens. Around 1813 this small group of Christians founded Seion, the first Baptist chapel in Llanelli. In 1822 John Roberts gave them a plot of land and the chapel was opened in June 1823. In May 1831, approval was given for independence from Adulam and 161 people transferred their membership to the new chapel at Zion. The membership grew and a new building was completed in 1858. In 1874 a new schoolroom was added.

Siloam Chapel, New Street, Kidwelly, *c.* 1906. The Baptist faith had its beginnings in Kidwelly in the late eighteenth century. The Revd Josiah Wilkins of Carmarthen, under whose able ministry two churches had been established at Llangyndeyrn and Ferryside, preached regularly in the town and the first Baptist chapel had opened by 1821. The work continued to flourish in the nineteenth century, and a new chapel was built on the old location. It opened in 1892 with a seating capacity of 500.

"Flee from the Wrath to Come."

SPECIAL

EVANGELISTIC SERVICES

Those who are anxious to obtain

FORGIVENESS OF SINS

Are invited to come to the

THEATRE, NEAR THE MARKET, LLANELLY.

Next SUNDAY, September 17th, 1882,

At 3 and 7 p.m., and also every night in the week at 7.30, when **Salvation as** offered by God in the **Scriptures** will be explained (D.V.) by

DAVID E. JONES,

Evangelist from Tredegar, and others.   ADMISSION FREE.

Gwahoddir pawb ag sydd eisiau

MADDEUANT PECHODAU A SICRWYDD O HYNY

I DDYFOD I'R **THEATRE**, LLANELLI.

DYDD SUL NESAF, am 3 a 7, a phob Nos yn yr wythnos am 7.30, pryd yr eglurir yr iachawdwriaeth o'r Beibl gan

DAVID E. JONES, Efengylydd o Tredegar, ac ereill.

"*Cyflog Pechod yw Marwolaeth, ond rhodd Duw yw Bywyd Tragywyddol.*"

MYNEDIAD I MEWN YN RHAD.

PRINTED AT THE GUARDIAN OFFICE, LLANELLY.

Poster of evangelistic meetings held by D.E. Jones at the Theatre, Cowell Street, 1882. Historically this poster heralded the beginning of the activity in Llanelli that led to the Gospel Halls of the movement popularly known as that of the Plymouth Brethren. David E. Jones was an evangelist from Tredegar who came to preach in Llanelli in 1882. In a booklet that he wrote later about his life, he says that the only place he could find was an old, vacated theatre. The *Llanelly and County Guardian* named this theatre as the Theatre in Cowell Street. People came in large numbers to his meetings so that he held four meetings a day. He held a Prayer Meeting in the morning, a Women's Meeting at 3.00 p.m., a Bible Reading at 6.00 p.m. and a Gospel Meeting at 7.30 p.m.

Evangelistic Hall, Arthur Street, *c.* 1930. In 1884 David Jones came again to preach in Llanelli, but this time he brought a tent. He concentrated his evangelistic activity in the Custom House Bank area, preaching the Gospel, visiting people in their homes and speaking to workers in the nearby docks. Later, he was able to use the offices of the Custom House. Mansel Rees of Cilymaenllwyd supported the work and used to travel on his horse along the beach to attend meetings. Converts were baptised in the Slip near the entrance to the North Dock. Eventually, land was acquired at the end of Robinson Street (the site is now in Arthur Street) and a church building was erected there.

Elders of the Evangelistic Hall, March 1982. From left to right: Gwyn Jenkins; Aneurin Evans; Willie Phelps; Herbert Board; Glyn Morgan; Glyn Christopher and Wynford Bowen. In 1982 the Evangelistic Hall celebrated its centenary from its beginnings in Custom House Bank and the commemorative booklet was written by Herbert Board.

Group from the Evangelistic Hall, Robinson Street, *c.* 1938. Regular open air Gospel meetings were conducted in west Wales. A coach would be hired and people would assemble in Robinson Street at 1.30 p.m. on a Saturday afternoon, many of them having worked on a shift in the tinworks before coming.

Gospel Mission from Llanelli, *c.* 1956. These regular evangelistic outings continued for many years when about thirty or forty men and women would travel to conduct open air Gospel meetings in places such as Haverfordwest, Tenby or Pembroke Dock, supporting this activity with the distribution of pamphlets outlining the Christian message of salvation in Jesus Christ.

Burry Gospel Hall, 1931. Back row: Will Thomas; Eddie John; Will Delaney; Luther Thomas. Middle row: Jack Jones; Magnus Bowers; Ted John; Sid Bryant. Front row: Jim John; Ivor Reynolds; Glyn Roberts. The growth in membership in the Evangelistic Hall led to evangelistic activity in the Machynis area that resulted in the building of the Burry Hall that opened in 1931.

Opening of Llwynhendy Gospel Hall, 14 March 1964. For years before this opening a Sunday school had been held in a local school in Llwynhendy and it was felt that there was sufficient interest to start a new church. Reg Bryant, a well-known local master craftsman and a member of Trimsaran Gospel Hall, was responsible for the building.

Salem Chapel, Felinfoel, *c.* 1914. Salem Chapel was an offshoot of Capel Newydd so the minister in Capel Newydd on Sunday morning would normally preach in Salem in the afternoon. In the late 1940s the evangelical Gladys Rees of the Forward Movement was allowed to hold regular mid-weekly services for children in this chapel building in which village children learned verses and stories from the Bible.

Salem Chapel, Felinfoel, annual Sunday School outing to Porthcawl, 23 July 1932. A day's outing in the year was a big event in the lives of chapel people and Porthcawl was one of the favourite places to visit from Llanelli.

The Salvation Army Band, Llanelli, 1909. In the late nineteenth century the new evangelical movement of the Salvation Army was concerned with the welfare of the poor in the growing industrial areas and they were established in Llanelli in 1882.

Salvation Army Citadel, Swansea Road, *c.* 1970. During 1915 the Salvation Army moved from Vaughan Street to the new Citadel in Swansea Road, which cost £1664. The building was opened by Sir Stafford Howard and had a seating capacity of 300 in the senior hall and 200 in the young people's hall. On the 7 June 1986, the Salvation Army moved to their new centre in Sunninghill Terrace.

A sampler worked by Mary Anne Phelps, aged thirteen, Llanelli, 1881. Many of the samplers produced by girls at school or at home have a Biblical theme with either a verse from the Bible or, as in this sampler, a related moral injunction.

five

People and Events

Visit of Lord Roberts to Llanelli to unveil the Soldiers Memorial, 26 August 1905. The Fallen Heroes Committee invited Lord Roberts to visit Llanelli and unveil a memorial to the local men who laid down their lives in the Boer War. On the day of his arrival decorations had been put up all along the route including a triumphal archway erected by the men of the 1st Welch. Even though it rained heavily, thousands of people turned out to see the ceremony and the former commander-in-chief in South Africa.

FALLEN HEROES MEMORIAL

Left: A life-size tinplate figure of Lord Roberts, Station Road, 1905. One of the most spectacular exhibits in the display erected for Lord Roberts was the life-size figure of himself on horseback on the tinplate archway opposite the works of Mr Trubshaw.

Below: Remembrance Card for William Stanley Williams, 1901. This card would have been produced by the family in remembrance of their son killed in the Boer (South African) War.

Opposite below: The Fallen Heroes Memorial, *c.* 1912. The memorial was first suggested by J. Allen Williams and the necessary funds were found from a subscription list opened in a local newspaper. The design of the memorial selected was that of Doyle Jones and represented a soldier with rifle in hand, ready for action. Postcards were soon on sale in Llanelli and, one, produced by Evans, printer, Llanelli – who produced a number of printed postcards of the event – gave the roll of the dead as: Corporals, Joseph Davies; Richard Howell,; Privates, E.R. Webb; Tom Owens; Samuel Smedley; Arthur Leonard and Trooper, Stanley Williams, Llanelly; Private John Jones, Llangennech; Private John Wales, Burry Port.

In Loving Remembrance

OF

WILLIAM STANLEY WILLIAMS,

SON OF JOHN AND LOUISA WILLIAMS, 2, LAKEFIELD PLACE, LLANELLY,

WHO WAS KILLED IN THE SOUTH AFRICAN WAR,
NEAR STANDERTON,

AUGUST 22ND, 1901,

AGED 21 YEARS.

LLANELLY
Great Kissing Competition

(By Moonlight   **By Special Desire).**

CLUB   BADGE.

⤳ RULES. ↢

Competitors must bring 2 lips (Tulips).
Must be over 7 and under 70.
Onions and peppermints strictly prohibited.

WILL YOU BE THERE?

Titchfield Series   Copyright.   No. 204

A comic postcard sold in Llanelli in 1909. In the Edwardian era postcards were produced on a vast range of subjects and comic cards were very popular. Generally these cards had a gentle humour and many, such as this card, were based on flirting or romance.

Llanelli Beach, *c.* 1912. This crowded beach gives a good indication of how popular the beach at Llanelli was. As was typical of the Edwardian period the women are in long dresses or skirts and wear hats, and many of the men are dressed in their best suits with bowler hats. Not one person can be seen in a swimming costume and there are only a handful of people who have ventured to paddle in the sea.

Gypsy encampment at Furnace, *c.* 1906. The gypsies camped near to Furnace Pond. The artist James Dickson Innes spent a lot of time with them during the time that he was painting the nearby Furnace Quarry.

Llanelli's first Borough Council, with H.W. Spowart (town clerk), Sir Stafford Howard KCB (mayor), and Alderman James Davies (deputy mayor), November 1913.

Llanelli Railway Strike Riots, Saturday, 19 August 1911. This historic photograph of the train stopped just before Union Bridge was taken soon after five marksmen of the Worcester Regiment under the command of Major Stuart had opened fire upon a crowd of people in or around the gardens of No. 4 and No. 6 High Street. In this shooting John John, who was a mill-worker at Morewood Tinplate Works, and Leonard Worsell, a Londoner who was lodging at No. 6 High Street, were killed in the garden of No. 6 High Street. John Francis of Glanmor Place had been shot through his neck and John Hanbury of Railway Terrace had been shot in the hand. At the time of the photograph the soldiers had been marched back to the station leaving the train abandoned. Above the embankment to the south the crowd are walking away from the back lane in Bryn Road.

Crowd being addressed at the eastern crossing of the station opposite the Railway Hotel, August 1911. On 26 August 1911, a Llanelli lady, Alice Rees, sent four postcards to a friend on which she wrote a lengthy note regarding the strike in Llanelli. This is an interesting contemporary view of the strike. On this, the first of her cards she wrote that, 'we have been so busy at the office what with holidays and strikes. The affair here was terrible. I suppose that you have already heard of all that happened last Saturday.'

Carriage windows smashed, 19 August 1911. At about 5.30 p.m. a train was stopped that had been carrying kit and provisions in the goods van for the Devon Regiment. The crowd went into a fury and flung the contents onto the line and broke every window. On this postcard Alice Rees continued, 'Just to give you an idea of the damage done. This of course is nothing compared to the trucks set on fire by the mob; and perhaps you can hardly believe it but the report is that there were not more than 50 roughs who played all the havoc. But the explosion was too terrible for words. I heard the report from the Post Office. I don't think I have ever felt so frightened in my life.'

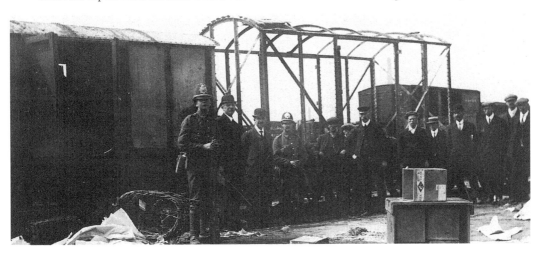

Police and railway officials guarding the wagons at the sidings including the van damaged in the explosion at Llanelli, 20 August 1911. The looting spread rapidly in the Goods Shed and the sidings and, altogether, about 96 trucks were looted. Between 11.00 p.m. and 11.30 p.m. two explosions were heard. A truck that had contained two cylinders of detonators and a box of carbide had blown up killing one person outright and fatally injuring three others. Alice Rees wrote, 'This is a snapshot my brother took last Sunday morning. This is the framework of the van which exploded with such awful results. But for all the horror it also had its humorous side. To see all the people carrying off the loot and to hear all they were saying was most amusing. There were many grand feasts of all kinds last Sunday.'

Soldiers and police with ransacked Buckley Brewery beer crates, 20 August 1911. In a fourth postcard Alice Rees described some of the looting that took place. She wrote that, '..by Monday the people began to get frightened when they knew the police were going around the houses making enquiries. There was tons of stuff thrown into the Bigyn School yard. But the soldiers are guarding it night and day now so that they have had to find a new place – St Paul's churchyard being the spot – or they bury it. One woman who had carted a lot of stuff from Thos Jones stores to Mincing Lane making several journeys when she thought she had enough went to look for it to take home (and) found it was all gone was heard to exclaim good heavens there's thieves about.'

A train stopped by strikers at Llanelli Station, August 1911.

Troops camping at Burry Port during the Llanelli riots, August 1911.

The Royal Sussex Regiment leaving from Burry Port Station, 24 August 1911.

Arthur John Davies MM, 1915. He was born in Alltiago Road, Pontardulais, on 17 November 1882. During the First World War he joined the 17th Battalion The Welch Regiment. The 17th Battalion was raised in Cardiff in early 1915 from men whose short stature would normally have debarred them from joining the army. As part of the 40th Division the Battalion moved to France in May 1916. On a night in July, 1917, he was involved in action with a raiding party consisting of two officers and forty-four other ranks in the vicinity of Gonnelieu. The party's objective was to examine the enemy's wire and defences but it was attacked by four separate parties and was involved in sharp fighting. During this action an officer was injured and L/Cpl Davies, together with two others, showed great gallantry in bringing the wounded officer back to the Battalion position. For this great gallantry he was awarded the Military Medal.

Left: Arthur John Davies, MM as postman in Dafen, *c.* 1955. The patch over his eye covered the wound he received during the First World War when he lost an eye as well as part of his skull. After the war he worked with the *Llanelli Guardian* and later became the village postman in Dafen. In his spare time he was very involved in promoting sport in the village, particularly the cricket club. Towards the end of his life he lived at Tir Capel, Dafen, until he died at the age of eighty on 4 December 1962.

Below: National Shell Factory, Llanelli, 1916. While many men were away fighting in the First World War a shell factory was set up at the Burry Extension Works in 1915. The factory employed mainly women who made the shells that were sent to the Royal Ordnance Factory at Pembrey.

Lady Catherine Meriel Howard Stepney with her daughter Marged, 1913. The wedding of Lady Stepney's daughter Meriel to Sir Stafford Howard KCB took place at the Parish Church on the 21 September 1911. Meriel Stepney was a very popular lady in the town and the people turned out in their hundreds to witness the wedding. A local paper said that although it was market day little or no marketing was done and business was practically suspended. The streets were decorated with bunting and the bells of the church pealed as she walked from her ancestral home Llanelli House to the church.. In 1913 their daughter Marged was born.

Above: Silver cradle presented to Sir Stafford and Lady Howard, *c.* 1913. Sir Stafford and Lady Howard were held in high esteem by the people of Llanelli who presented them with this handmade silver cradle to commemorate the birth of their daughter Marged Stepney Howard. The design of the cradle was by T. Vaughan Milligan who was Principal of the Llanelli School of Art. from 1911 to 1915. The cradle is an excellent example of local craftsmanship.

Right: Sir Edward Stafford Howard, KCB, Mayor of Llanelli, 1913-14. Sir Stafford Howard was born on 28 November 1851. He entered Parliament as a Liberal member for East Cumberland in 1876 and continued to represent that constituency until 1885 when he was elected for the Thornbury District of Gloucestershire. He was the Under-Secretary for State for India in Gladstone's government but in the 1886 election he was defeated and left Parliament for good. His first wife, Lady Rachel, daughter of the 2nd Earl of Cawdor, died in 1906 and he married Lady Stepney's daughter Meriel on 21 September 1911. He was the first Charter Mayor of Llanelly in 1913 and was re-elected in 1914 and 1915. He died at his London address, No. 11 Lowndes Square in 1916.

Parc Howard opening ceremony, 21 September 1912. Sir Stafford and Lady Howard made a handsome gift of the fine building Bryncaerau Castle and the twenty-four-and-a-half acres surrounding it to the Urban District Council of Llanelly for 999 years in trust for the inhabitants of the town and neighbourhood as a public park. It was formally opened and dedicated by them on the 21 September 1912, the first anniversary of their marriage. Hundreds of people watched the opening ceremony. The procession began at the Town Hall at 3.30 p.m. and proceeded along Stepney Street, Market Street and Thomas Street to the park. On arrival at the park, the chairman of the Urban District Council presented Lady Howard with a key, and, amidst loud cheers, she declared the park officially open. On the Dancing Green the Territorials formed a quadrangle inside which were about 4,000 children with all the girls dressed in white.

Bryncaerau Castle, c. 1912. In the year preceding the official opening of the park, great efforts were made to transform Bryncaerau Castle and its grounds, which had become quite dilapidated. A commemorative plaque in the building which now houses the fine Parc Howard Museum and Art Gallery states that: 'This building was renovated and the grounds surrounding it laid out as a public park and place of recreation by the inhabitants of the Urban District of Llanelly'.

Tennis courts, Parc Howard, *c.* 1912. On the day of the opening ceremony the park had four tennis courts including one of asphalt.

Bandstand, Parc Howard, *c.* 1916. The Howard Park Committee including Sir Stafford Howard KCB considered a number of designs for the bandstand before arriving at their decision; they also consulted Sergeant James Samuel, the conductor of the town band, as to the most suitable place in front of the castle for the creation of a stand. Eventually they decided that it should be erected in the middle of an area that they termed the Dancing Green.

Bowling greens' opening, Parc Howard, 1912. The Howard Park Committee were determined on getting high quality bowling greens for the park. In one of their meetings to consider the development of the park the deputy surveyor, J.H. Montgomery, had asked whether the committee would like to be advised by an expert in regard to turf for the bowling greens. There were, he said, some gentlemen in the town who were 'enthusiastic about bowls'. After some discussion the committee decided that, if possible, they should get sea-washed turf.

Mayor D.T. James JP at the International Bowling Tournament, Parc Howard, 1995.

Queen Elizabeth and the Duke of Edinburgh's visit to Parc Howard, June, 1977. The biggest crowd ever seen in Parc Howard greeted the Queen and the Duke of Edinburgh on their first visit to Llanelli since 1953. Some of the crowd of over 20,000 that packed the park had waited since 4.30 a.m.

Llanelly & Dist. Agricultural Horse Show Bank Holiday, Aug. 1st, 1921
FIRST PRIZE : TRADESMEN'S CLASS.

Above: Llanelli and District Agricultural Horse Show, 1 August 1921. The first prize in the Tradesmen's Class was won by Carmarthen United Dairies.

Left: Lloyd George at Llanelli Station, 11 November 1922. Visits by Lloyd George to Llanelli were always greeted with great enthusiasm by the people of the town. On 11 November 1922, there was a huge crowd outside the station waiting to see the ex-premier. On alighting from the train Lloyd George was introduced to Clark Williams, the Liberal candidate for the Llanelli Division. He was presented with a bouquet of white hothouse flowers and yellow chrysanthemums by Marged Stepney Howard (affectionately called 'Marged Fach' in the *Llanelly Mercury*), the daughter of Lady Howard, before being driven to address a meeting in support of the local Liberal candidate at the Market Hall. Thousands of people lined the route from Llanelli Station to the Market Hall to cheer him.

The declaration of the result of the general election on the steps of the Town Hall, 31 May 1929. The Conservative candidate Mr J.P.L. Thomas sat in a chair having hurt his leg, with Dr J.H. Williams the Labour victor on one side and Mr R.T. Evans, Liberal, on the other.

Llanelli children dressed in the national costume for the celebrations on St David's Day, photographed by J. Vaughan Evans, 1926.

Llanelly Star

WITH WHICH IS ASSOCIATED "THE BURRY PORT STAR."

General Post Office as a Newspaper,   SATURDAY, JUNE 8th, 1946

NDRY TO
RY ON

Efforts For
cial Aid

the town and particularly to the
Foundry to learn that, as a result
atives of the Glanmor Foundry Co.,
apartments, assistance is forthcoming

COLLIER WHO
FAILED TO
RETURN HIS LAMP

Beneath
Big Ben

Political Commentary

— By —

VICTORY MARCHERS

LLANELLY'S two fighting
units, the 484 S.L. Battery, R.A., and the 4th Batt.
Welch Regiment, are represented in the Victory March in
London by (reading left to
right) B.S.M. W. R. Basil
Evans, R.A., Sergt. W. J. P.
Evans, M.M., and Sergt. H.
Browning.

EN
S

Indi

SO far
mi
general
meetings
R.T.M.
clared i
dation
meeting
which e
strike a
week an
ing diff
methods.
The
branches
Millaen
which
day.

LLANELLY AIMS
FOR TARGET
OF £600,000

MR. W. E. DAVIES, chairman
of the Llanelly and District
Savings Committee and a member
of the National Assembly, presiding
at a meeting of 750 National Savings workers from East Carmarthenshire, at Felinfoel, said that

William John Phillip Evans, MM, 1946. In 1946 the *Llanelly Star* reported that Llanelli's two fighting units the 484th SL Battery RA and the 4th Battalion The Welch Regiment were to be represented in the Victory March in London and that William Evans was chosen as one of the three soldiers to represent the units. He was born in Llanelli in 1907, when his parents lived in Andrew Street. During the Second World War he served in the 4th Battalion The Welch Regiment. He displayed great gallantry and was awarded the Military Medal.

Opposite above: The official citation for the Military Medal award to W.J.P. Evans, 1945.

Opposite below: William John Phillip Evans' medals. His medals are mounted for wearing and include the Military Medal impressed on the rim 3958804 A/Sjt W.J.P. Evans Welch R, the 1939-45 Star, the France and Germany Star, the Defence Medal, the War Medal and the Efficiency Medal, Territorial with additional service bar 3958804 Cpl W.J.P. Evans MM Welch.

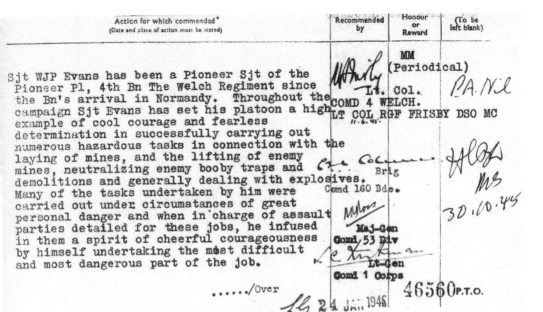

Action for which commended* (Date and place of action must be stated)	Recommended by	Honour or Reward	(To be left blank)

Sjt WJP Evans has been a Pioneer Sjt of the Pioneer Pl, 4th Bn The Welch Regiment since the Bn's arrival in Normandy. Throughout the campaign Sjt Evans has set his platoon a high example of cool courage and fearless determination in successfully carrying out numerous hazardous tasks in connection with the laying of mines, and the lifting of enemy mines, neutralizing enemy booby traps and demolitions and generally dealing with explosives. Many of the tasks undertaken by him were carried out under circumstances of great personal danger and when in charge of assault parties detailed for these jobs, he infused in them a spirit of cheerful courageousness by himself undertaking the most difficult and most dangerous part of the job.

......./Over

MM (Periodical)

Lt. Col.
COMD 4 WELCH.
LT COL RGF FRISBY DSO MC
11.6.45.

Brig
Comd 160 Bde.

Maj-Gen
Comd 53 Div

Lt-Gen
Comd 1 Corps

P.A. Nil

MB
30.10.45

46560 P.T.O.

24 JAN 1946

His devotion to duty was outstanding, particularly on one occasion in REUSEL, Holland when an R.E. party had been badly injured by drawing a minefield, without hesitation Sjt Evans took his assault section forward under heavy spandau and mortar fire, cleared the remaining minefield so that unit trucks were able to go forward.

This leadership and personal bravery and disregard to danger was a magnificent example to the remainder of the platoon and was undoubtedly largely responsible for the successes which they have had throughout the campaign.

Peace party celebration in Brynmelyn Avenue, Llanerch, 1945. At the end of the Second World War in 1945 there was great euphoria and parties were held in the streets to celebrate the occasion. The party in Brynmelyn Avenue was held in the square. Many of the children in this photograph would have experienced going to school carrying their 'Mickey Mouse' gasmasks and living under the threat of bombing but now they could dress up in the relaxed aftermath of the war.

Field Marshal, Viscount Montgomery's visit to Llanelli, 1948. A large crowd of people came to see Field Marshal Montgomery when he visited Llanelli towards the close of his tour of South Wales. He met the Territorial Association and civic and other dignitaries at the Drill Hall before going to the Town Hall. A local paper described the scene as reminiscent of cup final fervour or a royal visit as hundreds of people who had lined Murray Street and Station Road poured into Broadway to get as near as they could to the Town Hall. Here he is seen standing in the Victory Car as it passed the York Hotel from the direction of Broadway.

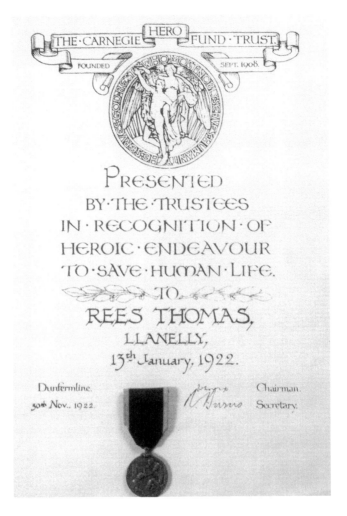

Edward Medal (Mines) to Rees Thomas, 1922. The Edward Medal for acts of gallantry in Mines and Quarries was instituted by a Royal Warrant of 13 July 1907. Depending on how the gallantry was assessed the recipient would be presented with a silver or a bronze medal which hung from a dark blue ribbon with a yellow stripe on either side. Both types were awarded very sparingly so the degree of gallantry required to be awarded a medal was high. Between 1912-30 only 134 bronze medals were awarded for gallantry in mines and one of these was to Rees Thomas. He was a miner employed at the Castle Colliery who, on the 13 January 1922, with two other miners named Meredith and Griffiths, was engaged in blasting operations with gelignite cartridges fired by time fuses. The fuses of the last three cartridges had been ignited, and the party was seeking safety when the cartridge fired by Meredith exploded prematurely, severely injuring him. Thomas with entire disregard to the danger to himself, at once went to his comrade's assistance, and dragged him back some little distance, but the remaining charges then exploded, injuring Thomas in the face and body. Meredith unfortunately succumbed to his injuries. Thomas' action in going back to rescue him when one shot had exploded and the other two were certain to do so was an extremely brave one, and he undoubtedly risked his life. He had also distinguished himself on the occasion of a previous accident. His medal, together with the Carnegie Certificate that he received, is in the Parc Howard Museum.

Left: T.V. Shaw with Clifford Evans *c.* 1950. T.V. Shaw was the headmaster of Llanelli Boys' Grammar School. Clifford Evans, the famous actor, was the son of Mr and Mrs D.H. Evans, Capel Road, Llanelli, and had been a pupil at the school where his acting abilities had been recognised. In the 1962 Eisteddfod at Llanelli he paid tribute to two of the teachers at the school, J. Afan Jones and Morgan Rees, who had given him the confidence to pursue an acting career.

Below: Coronation party in Robinson Terrace, later renamed Upper Robinson Street, 1953. A street party was organised in Robinson Terrace to celebrate the coronation of Queen Elizabeth in 1953. The children dressed up in costume for the occasion and they marched down Robinson Terrace and up Elizabeth Street as part of the celebration. The food was laid out on a table in the road under the shadow of the wall bordering the old gasworks. Part of the gasworks can be seen behind the large wall on the left.

Above: A marriage at Saron Chapel, Furnace, 10 June 1962. Ivor Bevan, a member of Capel Newydd married Gwyneth Davies, a member of Saron Chapel. The service was conducted by Saron Chapel's minister, Revd J.D.H. Evans. Revd C.M. Evans, the minister of Capel Newydd and William John Lewis, senior deacon at Capel Newydd and the groom's uncle, stand at extreme poles in this image.

Below: H.P. Wilkins and Arthur Mee, *c.* 1925. Hugh Percy Wilkins (1896–1960) who lived in James Street and Bradford Street, was a famous astronomer and cartographer with a special interest in the moon. He produced one of the most detailed maps of the moon before the start of the space age and one of the craters (Wilkins) on the southern uplands of the Near Side is named after him. In 1954 he was an Astronomical League Award winner. Arthur Mee who was an amateur astronomer also had a crater (Mee) named after him. In 1888, he published a book on the history and records of Llanelli Parish Church with notes relating to the history of the town.

William John Davies and Sarah Ann Harries were married at Capel Newydd on 26 December 1928.

Mrs W.J. (Nancy) Davies, 1985. Mrs Davies, a seamstress, spent a great deal of time making quilts that were sent to missionaries from the Evangelistic Hall, Arthur Street. She also enjoyed making models from materials about Llanelli's history: This model of a butcher's shop with numerous pieces of meat in the open air shows how such a shop looked in her young days in the early twentieth century.

Mr and Mrs Davies celebrated their Diamond Wedding on 26 December 1988, when they were visited by the Mayor and Mayoress, Mr and Mrs W. Mathonwy Jones.

 E R

23 December 1988

```
TELEMESSAGE LXP            ROYAL-CARD
MR AND MRS WILLIAM JOHN DAVIES
24 ELIZABETH STREET
LLANELLI
DYFED
SA15 1TP


    I SEND YOU BOTH MY WARM CONGRATULATIONS ON YOUR DIAMOND WEDDING
    ANNIVERSARY, TOGETHER WITH MY BEST WISHES FOR A HAPPY CHRISTMAS
    AND A MOST ENJOYABLE DAY.


    ELIZABETH R.
```

The message from the Queen, dated 23 December 1988, that Mr and Mrs Davies received congratulating them on their anniversary.

The National Eisteddfod in the old Market Pavilion, 1903. This was the second time that the eisteddfod had been held in Llanelli and was described as a great success. A local newspaper stated that Llanelli had given the Principality an example of 'how to do it'.

The Gorsedd procession marching along the new road at Frederick Street during the Royal National Eisteddfod of Wales at Llanelli, 1930. In the distance can be seen the Town Hall.

The Archdruid and the flower-dance girls at the Royal National Eisteddfod, 1962. The National Eisteddfod was held in Llanelli and, in spite of the bad weather, was described in a local newspaper as being one of the best nationals of the century.

Musicians at the proclamation ceremony of the Royal National Eisteddfod, 1962.

Lady Howard Stepney receiving the Freedom of the Borough, 1934. The year was the celebration of the twenty-first anniversary of Llanelli's incorporation as a borough and advantage was taken of the occasion to confer upon Lady Howard Stepney the Freedom of the Borough. This was a very popular decision as she was, quite deservedly, described in a local newspaper as 'Lady Bountiful'. The Town Hall was decorated with flags and streamers and large crowds were lined around its railings to watch the various guests arrive. There was a specially loud cheer when Lady Howard Stepney arrived accompanied by Mr Stafford Howard Stepney.

Freedom of the Borough being conferred on Alfred Daniell by the Mayor Cllr Roland P. Jones, 1925. Seated left is the Town Clerk H.W. Spowart and to the right the Deputy Mayor John L. Jones. Alfred Daniell was an eminent chemist and an old pupil of Copperworks School during the time of the headmaster John E. Jones.

Left: Programme for the Llanelly Choir at Windsor, 1907. In obedience to the Royal Command, the Llanelly Choir sang at Windsor Castle on 13 November before the King and Kaiser. As the choir left Llanelli Station for Windsor they were given a great send off as the platform was crowded with friends and well wishers. The *Llanelly Guardian* proudly asserted that this was the first occasion that a mixed choir had been in command at Windsor and that the choir of 230 voices marked a new epoch in the choral singing of Wales. All the male choristers wore white Windsor ties and the ladies were dressed in white.

Below: Ticket for Windsor, 1907. This ticket of admission with a wax seal was given to Rees Davies of Halfway who was one of the committee members. A small commemorative gold medal was also struck for this event which would have been awarded to certain key members.

YMWELIAD
Cymdeithas Gorawl Llanelli
A CHASTELL WINDSOR.

Rhaglen.

Mercher, Tachwedd 13, 1907.

CHOIR SOUVENIR PROGRAMME.

WINDSOR   CASTLE.

Admit Mr Rees Davies.
engaged in the Concert given by the Llanelly Choir at Windsor Castle on Wednesday 13th November 1907.

Entrance, North Terrace.

Demick Pratt

at the MANSION HOUSE
PARC HOWARD
LLANELLI

DAILY 2-8 May 3-17, 1969

AN EXHIBITION OF PAINTING SPONSORED BY LLANELLI
ART SOCIETY

Left: Catalogue of Exhibition of paintings by Derrick Pratt, Parc Howard, 1969. Derrick Pratt was one of the most important and influential artists in Llanelli during the early and mid-twentieth century. He was born in Walsall, Staffordshire in 1895, the son of the painter Edward Derrick Pratt. He studied at Leeds College of Art from 1911-15 and then served in the Royal Garrison Artillery from 1915-19. Following the war he was at the Royal College of Art from 1919-23. In 1923 he was appointed the Principal of the Llanelli School of Art and continued in that position until 1960. During this time he was the visiting art master at Llanelli Boys' and Girls' Grammar Schools from 1923 to 1938. His work was exhibited at the Glyn Vivian Gallery, Swansea and in various exhibitions through west Wales. In 1935 he had a painting exhibited at the Royal Academy in London.

Opposite above: Thomas Roberts' children, *c.* 1900. Sarah Roberts (seated left) was well known for her painting of cockerel plates in the South Wales Pottery, Llanelli. During her life she worked for about forty years in the pottery. She was a kind, popular woman known affectionately to everyone as Aunty Sal. She died on 19 November 1935, at the age of seventy-six.

Opposite below: A cockerel plate, South Wales Pottery, *c.* 1900.

Right: Dai Bach by Walter Cole, *c.* 1940. Walter Cole was fascinated by people who did unusual jobs, such as Dic Shrimps a man described elsewhere in this book as a seller of shrimps in the Machynis area. This painting of a cleaner in one of the billiard halls is entitled on the reverse *Dai Bach.*

Opposite Above: Walter Cole, Self Portrait, *c.* 1950. Walter Cole who lived at No. 1 Als Street was a talented artist. He was a bachelor who lived for art. He was a plasterer by trade but he painted prolifically and studied art in his spare time. Artist John Bowen described him as a fascinating character and a mine of information about the art of painting. Such was his interest in art that, as a young man he would cycle to Swansea to attend classes at the Swansea School of Art. As an older man Walter Cole would join the younger students in the evening Life Drawing classes at the Llanelli School of Art. At the models' rest time the students would enjoy listening to Walter's views and comments about painting in general and about the famous painters of the time. Some of Llanelli's most talented young painters of the time, Bromfield Rees, John Bowen and Robert Portsmouth, congregated in No. 1 Als Street where Walter Cole could show the drawings that he had been doing.

Opposite Below: Unveiling of a painting by Walter Cole at Parc Howard Museum, 1988. This is an important painting in the history of art in Llanelli as it portrays Henry Giles who was appointed the first principal of the Llanelli School of Art in 1907. Walter Cole had a high regard for Giles and said that he and other students, after classes, would walk to Llanelli Station with Giles (who lived at Carmarthen) when they would discuss art as they walked along the road.

Overleaf: Tony Evans, Nevill Gallery, 1975. Tony Evans (on the extreme right in the photograph) was born in 1920 in Broadway, Cardiff and only came to live in Llanelli in the mid-1960s when he took a job as a production engineer at the Morris Motor's Factory at Felinfoel. While at an art exhibition in Llanelli in 1968 he met Kathleen who was an accomplished sculptor in porcelain in her own right. They married and lived in a house in the Bryn overlooking the valley. He had a studio where he painted for hours every day especially after his retirement in 1981. Industrial life was to dominate most of his paintings and in these, the focus was on the men and women who worked in such difficult and dangerous conditions. He is best known for his paintings of tinworkers and miners whose lives at work and outside were painted with affection and an understanding of the conditions they worked under. The exhibition in 1975 was of, 'A Miner's Life'.

Tony Evans, Nevill Gallery, Llanelli, 1974. In 1974 Tony Evans had a one-man exhibition of Tin Workers at the Nevill Gallery in the Llanelli Library. In his paintings of tin workers he recorded a way of working that had disappeared with the advent of the mechanisation of the strip mills. He was very knowledgeable about the history of tinplate making and the processes involved and produced a small booklet about this.

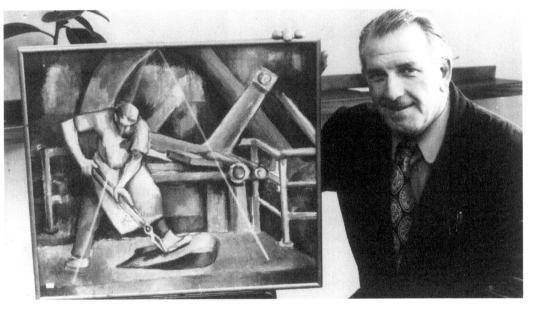

Tony Evans with his painting of *The Doubler*, 1974. Tony Evans did a series of paintings of men and women involved in the production line of a tinplate works which are now displayed in one room at the Llanelli Council Offices. This powerful painting of *The Doubler* painted with the dramatic, gleaming colours that was typical of his tinplate paintings, is the most well known of his paintings. The furnaceman heated the sheets and then passed them to the rollerman who inserted the sheets into the rolls. The sheet went through the rolls and the behinder passed it back to the Rollerman: this could happen several times. Following this the Doubler folded the sheets and placed them in the squeezer.

John Bowen, Sandy Road, 1998. John Bowen is one of the town's finest artists of the twentieth and early twenty-first centuries. He was born in Llanelli in 1914. He won a scholarship to the Llanelli School of Art and taught there from the age of nineteen. He became the art teacher at Llanelli Boys' Grammar School in 1939, but he continued to teach in the evenings at the Llanelli School of Art until the school moved to Carmarthen. He has often been asked to submit work to Arts Council Exhibitions in Wales and works by him are held by the Arts Council of Wales, the Newport Art Gallery and Museum and many other public collections. A fine collection of his work is held by the Parc Howard Museum and Art Gallery, Llanelli.

Llanelli Art Society award to John Bowen 1988.

John Bowen with painting of Spanish Gypsies, 1998. This painting was done with powerful, light colours, very different to some earlier paintings in which he used what he described as 'earth colours'.

The artist Vernon Hurford (seen here in 1980), who lived at Corporation Avenue, concentrated on fine line drawings of Llanelli's buildings. These were done from direct observation rather than from photographs. He was born in Neath in 1922, but his father, who worked on the railways, moved to a new job, and his family came to Llanelli in 1926. Vernon attended Old Road School where he was influenced by an excellent teacher of art and then he moved on to Stebonheath School where he won many prizes for art. In 1939 he started work in the town clerk's department at the Town Hall, but in 1940 signed up with the RAF and was posted as far afield as India and Burma during the Second World War. After the war he returned to the job he had left until he retired as assistant to the chief executive in 1981.

Island Place, June 1984. This drawing by Vernon Hurford captured a part of Llanelli that was about to change. The public house Island House remains, but all the little houses around have been demolished.

Unveiling of a Plaque on the wall of the birthplace of J.D. Innes, 27 February 1987. James Dickson Innes went to the Higher Grade School in the town before moving to Christ College, Brecon. From an early age he showed a talent in art and he became a student at Carmarthen School of Art as there was no such school in Llanelli at the time. In 1905 he commenced study at the Slade School of Art in London where he was a contemporary of Derwent Lees who became a great friend. During the first year he was one of two students to be awarded the prestigious Slade Scholarship which benefited him greatly through the academic years 1906–1908. Sadly, he suffered from poor health and he died at the young age of twenty-seven.

Above: Llanelli RFC, 1908. This was the team that defeated the Australian XV 8 – 3 in a historic match at Stradey Park on 17 October 1908. From left to right, in the back row are: T.R. Mills (chairman); Jim Watts; Jack Auckland; D. Llewellyn Bowen; A.J. Stacey; Will Cole; Ike Lewis; W.J. Thomas; and Tom Miller (committeeman). Middle row are: Handel Richards; Revd Tom Williams; Tom Evans (captain); Harvey Thomas and Will Thomas. Front row are: Dai Lloyd; Harry Morgan; Willie Arnold and W.H. Davies (trainer).

Below: Park Street Boys' School Rugby Team, 1925. This team was the winner of its league in the season 1924-25.

Above: Llanelli AFC, 1950/51. Formed in the 1890s, the club turned professional in 1912. In 1950 it gained re-entry to the Southern League, having dropped out of it in 1934. Jack Goldsborough had been the manager since 1934 – apart for a short period in the latter part of 1948 to January 1949 – and Jock Stein (who like Doug Wallace had played for Albion Rovers) was the captain in the 1950/51 season. In December 1951, Jock Stein signed for Glasgow Celtic, and later became a Scottish football legend. From left to right; back row: L McInnes; R. Ainge; P. Atkinson; A. Jackson; A. Taylor; L. Emmanuel; J. Gallagher. Front row: J. Goldsborough; G. Lewis; D. Wallace; J. Stein (cptn); N. Fleck; W. Bird.

Below: Llanelli Steelworks AFC, 1924–25.

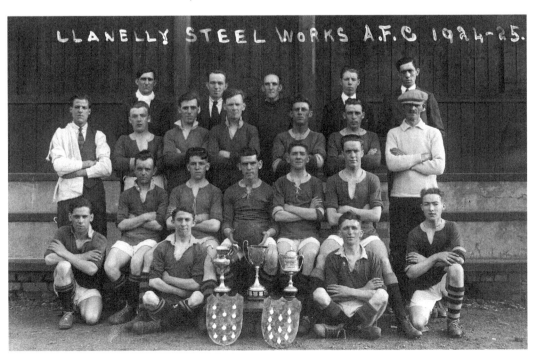

Grand County Match on Stradey Park, Llanelly,

SATURDAY, NOVEMBER 17th, 1883.
GLAMORGANSHIRE v. CARMARTHENSHIRE.

The following are the teams chosen to represent the respective Counties at the Grand Football Match to be played on Stradey Park, to-morrow (Saturday). The kick off will take place at 3 p.m, sharp. Admission, Sixpence.

Glamorganshire Team.	G.	T.	T.D.	Carmarthenshire Team.	G.	T.	T.D.
Back..........JONES, Pontardawe.....................				Back.........C. P. LEWIS, Llandovery............			
¾ Backs......S. S. CLARKE, Neath				¾ Backs......H. S. HOLME, Carmarthen..........			
,, ...F. F. PURDON, Swansea...........				,, ...PRICE JENKINS, Carmarthen......			
,, ...STEWART, Cardiff.....................				¼ Backs......D. H. BOWEN, Llanelly.....			
½ Back......CLARE, Cardiff..............				,, ...F. N. POWELL, Llanelly. ... ..,......			
¼ Backs......STADDEN, Cardiff...................				¼ Backs......F. L. MARGRAVE, Llanelly.........			
,, ...WILLIAMS, Neath...................				,, ...J. G. LEWIS, Llanelly............			
Forwards.. T. WILLIAMS, Neath				Forwards ..J. LLOYD, Carmarthen			
,, H. HINTON, Cardiff				,, HY. MITCHELL, Llanelly............			
,, LAYBOURNE, Cardiff.............				,, DD. WILLIAMS, Llandilo............			
,, WATKINS, Neath...................				,, THOMAS JONES, Llanelly...........			
,, ANDREWS, Swansea................				,, DAVID SMITH, Carmarthen			
,, RICHARDS, Swansea................				,, JOSEPH JOHN, Llanelly............			
,, MORGAN, Swansea................				,, GEO. LEWIS, Carmarthen			
,, LEWIS, Pontardawe................				,, A. SMITH, Llanelly............			

A Welsh Football Union Programme, 1883. This is an early and rare programme of a rugby match played at Stradey Park in 1883.

T. Evans of Llanelli (on the right) was the winner of the West Wales Open Bowling Championship, 1926.

Dafen Cricket Club, 1955. From left to right, in the back row are: David J. Daniels (chairman); Howard Morgan; Mervyn Jones; Raymond Lewis; Mervyn Morgan; Cliff Thomas and Arthur John Davies MM. (treasurer). In the front row are David Charles (secretary); Raymond Thomas; Rhydwyn Daniel; Glyn Davies (captain); Tommy Jones; Gwilym Williams; Gerwyn James and Edgar Andrews (committee man).

Hatchers Billiard Hall, Vaughan Street, c. 1938. This excellent, well-kept billiard hall was started by Fred Hatcher in 1932. He was a Devonshire man who became manager of the Lucania Billiard Hall before deciding to start his own club. In the early days fees were charged on a set basis (sixpence a set) but, later, this was changed to a time basis. The seven tables and the room in this photograph are immaculate and this is the way that it always was under the strict but fair discipline of Fred. The club fostered many champions including David Thomas who won the Welsh Boys' Snooker Championship in 1954. Later, it was into this hall that a young teenager named Terry Griffiths was to come to play and go on to become World Snooker Champion.

Terry Griffiths Matchroom, Town Hall Square, 26 June 2004. This building was the Ritz Dance Hall that was a popular venue for townspeople. In the rock and roll era of the 1960s it became the Glen which was a focal point for many people in Llanelli. The building was renovated and developed as a snooker hall and the Terry Griffiths Matchroom opened its doors in September 1987.

Above: John Pellew playing in the Terry Griffiths Matchroom, 26 June 2004. John Pellew plays for the club and is also a Welsh Snooker Referee.

Opposite: Terry Griffiths, 1994. Terry Griffiths who was born in Llanelli in 1947 is one of Llanelli's great sporting heroes. At the age of only sixteen he won the Llanelli and District Snooker Championship. In 1975 he won the Welsh Amateur Championship and in 1977 and 1978 the English Amateur titles. In only his second professional championship he won the World Snooker Championship in 1979 at the Crucible Theatre in Sheffield, when he beat Dennis Taylor by twenty-four frames to sixteen.

Terry
Griffiths

Other local titles published by The History Press

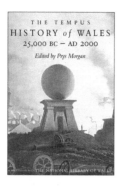

The Tempus History of Wales

PRYS MORGAN

Wales was at the heart of the Industrial Revolution, towns like Merthyr Tidfil driving the engine of the British Empire. The cultural and social divide between modern, industrialised Wales and the traditional agricultural areas is explored within this comprehensive volume.lurb

0 7524 1983 8

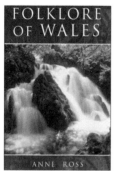

Folklore of Wales

ANNE ROSS

Wales is a Celtic country and the Celts have always treasured oral learning and recitation. Indeed they have a passion for committing facts to memory rather than relying on the written word. So it is no surprise, as we can see from Anne Ross' study, that the Welsh folklore and story-telling is so rich and varied.

0 7524 1935 8

Swansea Rugby Football Club 1873-1945

BLEDDYN HOPKINS

The 'All Whites' were founded in 1873 and became one of the eleven founder clubs of the Welsh Rugby Union in 1881. Swansea Rugby Club's history is renowned the world over for its many achievements. This volume traces the club's development from its formation through to the end of the Second World War. It gives a fascinating insight into the club and features team photographs, player portraits, action shots and many items of club memorabilia.

0 7524 2721 0

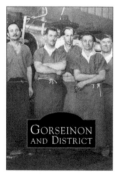

Gorseinon

KEITH E. MORGAN

This book charts the growth of Gorseinon and the surrounding district from a cluster of small agricultural hamlets into a thriving industrial community. It comprises over 200 archive images depicting all the different aspects of life in the area, from the pit winding gearand smoking chimneys of the local coal and steel industries to the dance bands and day trips out in the charabancs or half-cab coaches.

0 7524 2859 4

If you are interested in purchasing other books published by The Histoy Press, or in case you have difficulty finding any of our books in your local bookshop, you can also place orders directly through our website
www.thehistorypress.co.uk